ELIZABETH FRITSCH

PUBLISHED IN THE SAME SERIES

Alison Britton In Studio
A view by Peter Dormer and David Cripps

ELIZABETH FRITSCH

A VIEW BY PETER DORMER AND DAVID CRIPPS

BELLEW · LONDON

Published by Bellew Publishing Company Ltd
7 Southampton Place
London WC1A 2DR

ISBN 0 947792 04 X

Printed in Great Britain

CONTENTS

The changing role of craft 7
Elizabeth Fritsch: ideas and influence 11
The expressive pot 25
A biography 31
References 32
Index 96

Portrait of Elizabeth Fritsch taken at Digswell House, Hertfordshire

THE CHANGING ROLE OF CRAFT

Elizabeth Fritsch is the first of Britain's genuinely modern potters in that she was quick to understand the equivocal, yet potentially rich, position of artist and craftswoman that the twentieth century could provide. She has taken to pottery because it is a demotic language but she has used it as a vehicle for an aesthetic which has been largely structured by ideas and sources outside pottery.

Forms of pottery are almost as old as human culture itself, and pottery is a communal language because these forms are understandable across centuries and across cultures. For example, certain Korean and Chinese pots evoke similar sensations in a wide variety of people from different cultures—sensations of sheer aesthetic pleasure at such quiet delight and perfection in single simple artefacts. The domestic aspect of pottery reveals connotations of order, peace, security and harmony. In Elizabeth Fritsch's work there is a dialectic between such qualities and surprise, connotations of ritual and the surreal – an interaction between poetry and prose.

The current popularity of the craft object has much to do with the idea of having objects that are lively to the eye and to the touch, which yield something extra with every second glance, and yet are couched in familiar forms. To an extent craft objects offer reassurance: they are not questioning or polemical. And yet, at the same time, the existence and the persistence of men and women defying modern economic practice by lavishing both art and skill on single artefacts is a challenge to the status quo – an act of resistance against the pressure to conform with a cynical society that knows the price of everything and the value of nothing.

The contemporary artist in craft has found a role as a provider of solace and delight, but one should not infer that a proselytizing craft cannot exist. We have seen the applied arts put to proselytizing use in this century during the early years of the Russian revolution, when all art forms were enthusiastically pressed into ideological and revolutionary service.

The function of craft has become aesthetic rather than utilitarian. Of course, functional ware thrives as the growing number of domestic potters shows, but craft wares are bought not out of necessity but out of choice. The choice is for aesthetic value; function is well catered for by factories who produce their products more cheaply than any craftsman. And as the function of craft has veered towards aesthetics the points of contact between it and abstract fine art have become clearer. The finest pots and the best abstract art achieve and impart their beauty and demonstrate their humanity through their very forms – they are not about anything, they just exist and are complete in themselves. Fritsch points out that the finest of Hans Coper's pots can be compared to Brancusi's sculptures.

The greater the degree of aesthetic content of a craft object, the more questions arise in the course of its creation. Why this shape and not another? Why that material and not another? Previously such questions were answered by the dictats of function, but those dictats do not hold if the object is not for use. If the role of the crafts is largely aesthetic then what informs the aesthetic? Which traditions become the legitimate resource for the modern potter?

The creation of aesthetic objects does not, any more than does the creation of functional objects, often come healthily out of confusion or arbitrariness. Yet both these qualities seem at times to overwhelm modern crafts practice.

In the past the ornamental, religious, mystical and aesthetic aspects of craft were a response to demands of religious institutions or very small classes of wealthy patrons who knew what they wanted. Today's large constituency for 'craft as art' is diverse and uncertain about the criteria involved – and so, too, are many of the craftsmen. For the new revival in the crafts to establish itself into a firm and genuinely modern movement, critical evaluation and debate have to be encouraged.

The crafts world internationally is beginning to take stock of itself, and there is a lot of stocktaking to do. There is much to be done in simply writing a history of craft to see how we arrived at the point where we find ourselves now. For example, in spite of several interesting books about the Bauhaus, the relationship of the Bauhaus to crafts, and crafts to the modern movement, still needs to be explored. The split between modernism and the crafts may not be so complete as has been assumed. And, because all of us have access to the cultures of the world through museums, films and books, there is a need, too, for critical vigilance to prevent a cultural cacophony diffusing the crafts into kitsch. Consequently, questions tumble over themselves about current craft practice, and craft will be strengthened if they are answered and debated.

As we look at Elizabeth Fritsch's pots, we can see a number of diverse sources that influence their making. She says that there are so many things that astonish her in the world that: 'I create in astonishment and I hope to communicate that astonishment through my work.'

'Vase', Lucie Rie, (Austria-Britain), stoneware, 1976 h26cm. Lucie Rie's impact on British studio pottery has been as strong as Coper's but she is much more of an ornamentalist potter and makes no claims towards 'sculpture'

'Fish Bottle', Bernard Leach, stoneware, 1970 h38cm. Leach made about fifty of these bottles. Leach was the father of British studio pottery in the twentieth century and he established in Britain the idea that the potter could be an 'Artist' and not just a craftsman. He was hugely influential, but later generations of potters have reacted against the Anglo-Oriental 'tradition' which Leach contrived

'Stoneware Pot', Hans Coper, (Germany-Britain), stoneware, 1972 h22cm. Hans Coper's inspiration came from several sources including Cycladic sculpture. His influence on the younger Post-war potters was considerable, but, unlike Bernard Leach, Coper spawned few direct imitators. He was a catalyst for ideas rather than a propagandist for a single aesthetic ideology. Much of Coper's work exists in the borderland between pottery and sculpture – he was one of the very few studio potters whose work had a content, most frequently sexual

'Bottle', stoneware, Michael Cardew, 1924 h17cm. Cardew was Leach's first and most important pupil and almost equally influential. His long periods in West Africa introduced elements of African pottery style into his and his followers' work

ELIZABETH FRITSCH: IDEAS AND INFLUENCES

Elizabeth Fritsch is an independent as well as an original potter. Although she has naturally been influenced by pots and art from other cultures, she is not an imitator. Her originality as a potter stems partly from the fact that she draws her ideas from other disciplines such as music, literature and philosophy.

She sees herself as a 'painter who makes pots', but she would not want you then to infer that she belittles pottery in deference to painting. The difference between craft and art, as she sees it, is that the one is repeatable, the other not. She wants to make unrepeatable artefacts: she demands the language of crafts with the content of art.

Fritsch was drawn to pots and painting while studying music in London at the Royal Academy of Music. She became a close friend of stage-set designer Joseph Carl, who was 'immensely knowledgeable' about the visual arts, and together they visited galleries and museums throughout London, Amsterdam and Paris. Ancient pots attracted her. 'I owe a lot to Greek Bronze Age pots and Islamic pots but I was also impressed by Lucie Rie and Hans Coper.' Lucie Rie was one of the first potters to develop an alternative route in pottery in the face of the Leach orthodoxy. Fritsch also talks of the charisma of old pots and the attraction of archaeology – the discovery of archetypes – and it is an interest which partly explains the appeal of Coper's pots. 'I think Coper is daring. He managed to make pots that were both archetypal pots and sculptures at one and the same time.'

Elizabeth Fritsch has plenty of ideas to feed her creative impulse, and although she is inspired by other artists and by craftsmen of the past she has no need to imitate them. This attitude or gift is rarer in contemporary English pottery than it is in, say, that of the United States.

In England twentieth-century studio pottery derives chiefly from the work of Bernard Leach, who spent ten years (1909-20) in Japan; on his return to England he drew his inspiration from the many Oriental pots he had collected. Leach knew much more about the Orient than he did about British pottery of the time and his propaganda for the 'Eastern approach' of combining art with utility in Oriental-style wares gave British pottery a narrow focus for several decades. Leach had many imitators but, although he is himself correctly credited with some fine work, the pots of his imitators reveal their superficiality when compared to Korean or Japanese originals. A reaction against Anglo-Orientalism began in Britain in the 1950s, only to be replaced by a Scandinavian influence.

The two outstanding potters in England in the period after the Second World War were the expatriates Lucie Rie (from Austria) and Hans Coper (from Germany), neither of them reacting with or against a parochial Anglo-Orientalism. They were outsiders, and Fritsch, heir to Coper, is an outsider as well—not because she is a foreigner but because she brings to pottery an intellectual bias and because her own emotional roots lie in music and mathematics. She is, in a sense, a model of the urban potter in the twentieth century and something of a surprise to people who insist that wine jars and beer jugs are the proper work of the potter. Although Elizabeth Fritsch owes ideas to other sources, she sets her own goals rather than tries to work up to someone else's.

When she first applied to the Royal College of Art she was turned down—this was in 1966, when she had finished her studies as a musician. David Queensberry, who was Head of Ceramics at the Royal College of Art, explained some years later: 'We could be forgiven for not taking her in 1966 as she had virtually no work to show us, only a few pots that had been given a very low biscuit firing, perhaps alongside a baked potato. Despite the fact that her work was minimal and showed little technical understanding of the subject, one was aware of a most unusual sensitivity. She had thought more than most people and from an intellectual and spiritual point of view was in a completely different category from most of the students who applied to us.'[1] She was admitted second time round in 1967, although with barely more work in her portfolio.

Once at the Royal College Fritsch was helped by Hans Coper, a part-time tutor, and she also had many conversations with the artist Eduardo Paolozzi. Fritsch says that Coper and she became friends partly because they both disliked the oatmeal ruralist fashion in pottery and both hated what Coper called 'galumphing studio pots'—English pots derived from

Scandinavian work. It was Coper who helped Fritsch develop her understanding of how to paint pots and encouraged her early experiments with geometrical rhythms and colour.

Geometrical rhythms

In her essay accompanying the exhibition of her pots, 'Pots About Music' (1978-79), Fritsch explains that a key point in her pottery was the work she did for her first one-person show at the Crafts Council in 1974: 'Geometric rhythms became more rigorous and spatial games took over both in the painting and in the forms themselves, which started to become foreshortened, inhabiting the shadowy space halfway between two and three dimensions...I like the surreal and insubstantial feeling it gives to a form-giving it, in a very literal sense, "edge".'

Painting is a medium dealing in illusory space – a world imagined beyond the flat plane of the picture. Pottery, modelling and sculpture use real space and real volumes. Putting illusory space on top of forms with real volumes creates possibilities, and not the least of these is the fixed viewpoint. All paintings to some extent dictate the viewpoint from which they are to be seen. In a painting that uses two-point perspective the viewpoint is fixed precisely. But with a pot or a sculpture you can walk around it and view it from any number of points. How can you create a coherent, multi-faceted painting? And, what is more, painting on to a three-dimensional object can easily alter the way we read its shape and volume.

Having painted watercolours for more than a decade, Fritsch began painting pots while she was at the Royal College of Art. On the first pots the painting was not moved and modified by the form. Hans Coper suggested the pot should have more influence on what was painted on it. What Fritsch wanted was an integration between form and painting; she did not want any sense of the painting being an applied decoration, nor any superficial prettiness. 'Hans helped me to paint such that it was rhythmic and integral to the pot.' At the same time she began exploiting the paradoxes that are possible once illusory space is nudged ever closer to real space and especially the paradoxes that occur when you present the real as illusory and the illusory as real. Take *Optical Cup* (1975) as an example (page 17). Here is a cup which is elliptical, not circular. From real life we know that round things such as cups and bottles look elliptical at the top when seen from certain angles. The *Optical Cup* is formed so that from one viewpoint it will look as though it is fully round, and the painting around the rim confirms this. But this 'trick' is the least interesting aspect of the pot and certainly not its *raison d'être*. The more interesting aspect is the interplay between the different optics. For example, the handle of the cup is in a different optic from the body and thus throws the cup into ambiguity. The interplay of the optics creates a sensation of disembodiment especially as there is, too, that enigmatic, Piero della Francesca hued, painted cube on the front.

The cube implies a totally different kind of space from that occupied by the cup as a whole. Here we see an instance, of which we shall see more later, where geometry is used as a poetic device. It is emblematic and makes the cup seem incorporeal. Geometry is part of Fritsch's poetry of astonishment.

Astonishment is the quality she most wants her work to communicate to people – it is the sensation of surprise that is perhaps in part a shock of recognition, the discovery of something wondrous which you 'knew' all along. It is the excitement that is the province of anyone discovering something good, be it a mathematical formula or the very particular blue of an Aegean sky. The spatial games combined with the 'celestial' colours she uses are a way of making surprising objects.

What she is creating with her geometries is a form of minimal surrealism. She says:...'the paradoxical movement away from the substantial (clay pot) towards the insubstantial (air and music) obsesses me. The most haunting paintings are those that have an optical surrealism: an inclination towards the insubstantial...the paintings of William Blake (1757-1827) and the famous painting *The Ambassadors* by Holbein (1533), in the foreground of which floats a skull which, unlike the rest of the picture, is painted in a mysterious 2½-dimensional optic... Ideally, I would like the optical illusionistic pots to have an emblematic function similar to that of Holbein's skull.'[2]

Holbein's skull

Fritsch is impressed by John Berger's analysis of the Holbein painting.[3] Berger says every inch of the painting appeals to the sense of touch: 'The eye moves from fur to silk to metal to wood

14

'The Ambassadors', Hans Holbein the Younger, *reproduced by
courtesy of the Trustees, The National Gallery, London*

15

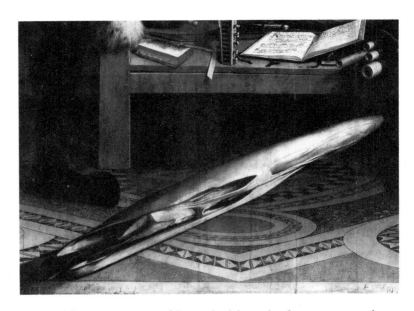

to marble to paper to felt and although the two men have presence it is the material surrounding and clothing the men that dominates.' (Note, too, that the appeal to touch in Fritsch's own work is a key quality.)

Among other things, *The Ambassadors* suggests the desirability of money because money buys things which are tangibly desirable. However, there in the foreground of the painting is the skull – the mysterious oval slanting form. Berger points out, 'What is significant is that the skull is painted in a literally different optic from everything else in the picture. If the skull had been painted like the rest, its metaphysical implications would have disappeared.' The skull is a reminder of mortality, it subverts the tangible materialism by reminding us that it and ourselves are temporary. (Of course, a *memento mori* can be dual edged, and more expedient individuals might say that a reminder of their mortality actually enhances the commodity value of earthly wealth – take and enjoy it while you can.)

The incorporeal nature of the Holbein skull derives from its projection, its optic, which demands of the viewer that he or she look obliquely at the painting to make out what it is. Such an oblique look is a metaphor, it parallels the same oblique look or questioning of assumptions that is required if what we take for granted in real life is to be re-evaluated. By taking 'oblique' looks, we also discover more that is astonishing.

'Optical Cup', stoneware,
1975 h14cm

The use by Holbein of an emblem in a different projection naturally intrigues Fritsch since most of her work explores several different projections and is emblematic in the sense that she uses geometrical ploys to twist pots into an interplay between the commonplace and the metaphysical. Just as the Holbein is full of material familiarity, so too is Fritsch's work instantly familiar, the forms are pot-like, but through her geometries she can turn the familiar into a surprise. The key word for Fritsch in this is 'dialetic' – she heightens the surreal aspect to a pot and this is played off against the pot as a commonplace fact. Thus they become emblems in the real world.

The surreal

The particular link Fritsch has with the surrealist movement is the pursuit of 'the marvellous'. The French poet and leader of surrealism, André Breton (1896-1966), said, 'The marvellous is always beautiful, anything marvellous is beautiful, in fact only the marvellous is beautiful...'.[4] Fritsch's route to evoking this quality touches surrealist practice at several points. One of them is colour. Colour for Fritsch is the most important aspect of painting and it seems to have an hallucinatory, other-worldly power for her, as is suggested by her description of the West of Ireland coast: 'An extraordinary landscape with its feeling of being only just in this world; the sea-shore colours and the mountains light and airy, are reflected in the magical folk music and in the old weaving with its celestial colours.'[5]

The surrealists believed or said they believed that the surreal world does exist – they used their art to reveal to us tangible evidence of the existence of that surreal world. Just as scientists use mathematics to 'bring back' evidence of the real world of quantum physics (a real world with as much reality for most of us as the Olympian world of the Gods) artists discover 'the marvellous' through their art. Fritsch's work can be seen in this light – her pots are discoveries.

The fascinating aspect of surrealism is the fact that the sensation or experience of beauty is non-intellectual – you experience it unequivocally, unmediated by thought. However, the route to the discovery, the creation of the art which reveals beauty, is multi-faceted and dependent upon many various sources and ideas. The goal is pure sensation but the path may need much erudition; that too appeals to Fritsch.

Labyrinths

Among the most original of the surrealists is the Argentine writer Jorge Luis Borges (b. 1899). If one were to describe Fritsch's output in art historical terms, a division could be drawn between pots that are post Borges and those that are not.

Borges finds metaphysics attractive but he turns it, and also mathematics and religion, into elegant games of the mind. As in the best games, the details are precise and believable and there is always a deep logic at work. Borges frequently tells his stories as though they were reports and the stories become a collusion between writer and reader – they are very much fact and fiction interpenetrating and the incredible becomes credible. Fritsch says, 'I was astonished and captivated by Borges stories, which I discovered in 1969, but I did not think about them in relation to my work until about 1980. It was the art critic Edward Lucie-Smith who led to my thinking about Borges in relation to my work when he wrote that my pots were "like evidence of an imaginary society". And the story that came strongly to my mind was *Tlön, Uqbar, Orbis Tertius* – a story about an imaginary society.'

Tlön, Uqbar, Orbis Tertius is an ironic interplay between fact and fiction, and Fritsch sees some of her recent work, which refers to this and other fictions by Borges, as providing some extra tangible evidence from some of his fictional locations (but not illustrations of the stories). In *Tlön* the narrator reports on his gradual discovery of a totally new world. The report proceeds via glimpses and whispers – a curious note in an encyclopedia here, the discovery of two or three clay urns there – and gradually the new world is offered up to the reader as an idea to turn over in the mind. And the new world that is uncovered is one in which each person creates and improvises his or her own reality. Poignant and evocative ideas emerge, 'Things become duplicated in *Tlön*; they also tend to become effaced and lose their details when they are forgotten. A classic example is the doorway which survived so long as it was visited by a beggar and disappeared at his death. At times some birds, a horse, have saved the ruins of an amphitheatre.' *Tlön, Uqbar, Orbis Tertius* is a tale with especial significance for artists because they are creators of new objects and guardians of old ones. Similarly, objects are created in the story by a process of improvisation – as in art.

It would be easy to misinterpret Fritsch's relationship to Borges's work. She is not seeking to illustrate his work, nor is she trying to weave wordy ideas around her pots to justify them; she would simply like to join in the ironic game he plays. When she makes the pots she is acting as 'archaeologist', making pieces of evidence for an imaginary world. And, of course, Fritsch's pots provide an experience of aesthetic pleasure which does not depend upon the mediation of theory, words or intellectual analysis. Nonetheless, the artist or the potter's route to creating work need not be direct and is unlikely to be without intellectual inspiration. It has been said of Borges that his erudition is vast but not profound and that he asks of it only flashes of lightning and inspiration. A similar relationship between their erudition and their creative work undoubtedly holds for many artists, including Fritsch. Her pots are not hard to understand or enjoy but they derive their coherence and interest from the variety of Fritsch's interests; and it is equally true that those who want to follow Fritsch's ideas can do so, and the complexity of interest is an addition to the original and continuing pure enjoyment of the work.

What are the coincidences of sensibility between Borges and

Fritsch? Both share a delight in things that are incorporeal; both prefer the intimate scale – Borges writes short fiction and poems, not novels, and Fritsch produces pots; both explore the precision of geometry and logic in their work; they share a similar sensibility for colour; and in both cases their work is enriched by a cosmopolitan, multi-ethnic and eclectic diet of cultures. For Borges this diversity has meant a wide reading of the world's literature, and for Fritsch a receptiveness to a variety of ethnic music and pottery.

The landscape of music

While the interests of Borges and Fritsch coincide, music is Fritsch's real landscape. She studied the harp and the piano at the Royal Academy of Music, and classical music, especially Bach, was one of 'three exciting things I did meet at school which have had a permanent hold on me'. The other two were geometry and Greek mythology.

The possibility of combining sound and sight, time and space, and music and colour is one of Fritsch's major preoccupations, stemming from around 1978, when she prepared the collection of pots shown in the exhibition 'Pots About Music'.[5] This interest in synaesthia (whereby one can 'hear' colours and 'see' sounds) has deepened: among her recent pots with an overt reference to music is *Hexagonal Jar: From Nowhere Street* (page 37), which refers to a piece of music called 'Nowhere Street' by composer and saxophone player Steve Lacey.

Her commitment to music shows a preference for the Ideal – music is an idealist and non-representational art. It is the art to which other arts have often been said to aspire.

The twentieth century has seen many attempts by artists to capture some of music's power in their own work – notably Wassily Kandinsky (1866-1944) the Russian-born pioneer of abstract art, Bauhaus teacher and an intense believer in the correlation between colour and sounds and the practical possibility of expressive abstract colour painting speaking directly, like music, to the soul. Kandinsky is a favourite of Fritsch's.

But synaesthesia as a concept falls down whenever it is claimed that any spectator will share with any other spectator the same emotions as the result of a particular combination of colour or sound. Some artists, such as Kandinsky, have a special ability to translate from one sense to another automatically – it is recorded that Kandinsky felt some colours as strongly as others feel sounds. Fritsch, too, feels strong connections between music and the colours and movements she has painted on to her pots. (Among her other favourite artists is the Russian painter Kasimir Malevich.) Some of her pots such as *Optical Pot* (1976, page 50) are the results of collaboration with the jazz composer Veryan Weston but in recent years Fritsch has not had the opportunity to work closely with a musician. On the matter of how much musical content a spectator is expected to see in these pots she says: 'One can only say these pots were made with the intention of being about particular composer's music.'

There is, however, an analogy between reading patterns and listening to music which is relevant to Fritsch's pots. Several people have said, notably E H Gombrich,[6] that, if we look at a pattern, whether it be simple or complicated, we have to read it, we do not take it in at one go. Reading a pattern depends upon both memory and anticipation, a sense of past, present and future. Even if we are simply reading a row of dots we have to be able to remember what we have just seen in order to compare it with the one we expect. This, says Gombrich, is similar to our perception of rhythmical sounds: 'The idea of rhythm depends on the memory of a time interval and our ability to hold this memory in anticipation of the next sound.'

The importance of this comparison between pattern-reading and music for Fritsch's pots can be seen by looking at her work and by recalling the emphasis noted earlier that she places upon geometric rhythms.

There are other links between music and visual artefacts. Music provides a rich language of metaphor which critics use in their descriptions of art as their natural language of description. The descriptive language music offers is particularly appropriate to Fritsch's pots and, as she says, the basis of the musical equivalence in her work stems from the fact that she regards the form of a pot – such as *Spout Pot From Tlön* (on page 79) – as providing the melody with the colour being the harmony.

In her 'Pots About Music' catalogue Fritsch writes: 'The geometric tonal structures and rhythm figures in music have a flowing dynamic vitality – a kind of levity, which corresponds with my rhythmic and geometric aspirations of painted colour on a form.' Later, she says: 'The spaces between pots assembled in groups (whether side by side or overlapping in the distance) is to me more lively and musical than any of the spatial relationships which may be incorporated in an individual piece.' This, too, bears out what Gombrich says, since apprehending a group of Fritsch's pots is indeed a matter of 'reading' and understanding one thing in relationship to another.

The grouping of pots is very important with Fritsch's work; it is a key reason for having exhibitions because it gives her the opportunity for group improvisation (by the same token it also means that it is only partly accurate to categorize her pots as a domestic art form since it is most likely that such improvisation in groups is possible only in exhibition spaces). Assembling the pots into groups is for her like improvised music; it is a 'free' activity but at the same time disciplined by the nature of the individual components.

THE EXPRESSIVE POT

'There is a paradox involved between real and surreal function; between kitchen and temple; between ordinary prosaic fact and an exciting poetic metaphor. All good pots belong to some extent to both worlds...'. Thus Elizabeth Fritsch outlines her ambitions for her own work. Good work in craft or art or design is possible when the craftsman/artist/designer is alive to the fact that whatever he or she makes contains the possibility of metaphor.

Every art medium has its particular strengths, and, although pots are like paintings or sculpture in that these forms cannot state ideas (as can the novel or play), pottery is nevertheless a rich medium. The possibility of metaphor and poetry in pottery is vast once it is recalled how varied the roles of pots have been in the history of man. Pots communicate primarily and substantially at the level of pure sensation rather than conceptually, although much depends upon the context in which the pot is presented. And while Fritsch makes many conceptual demands on herself, her pots do not necessarily make such demands on her audience.

Fritsch has a clear idea about the nature of her work. She says of her pots that the only essential physical function they express is the 'minimal one of containing'. But the fact that she makes vessels is important: it is a 'function' which provides a formal coherence and discipline for her as an artist, and it is a strong point of contact for the audience. There are allusions to abstract ideas – allusions carried through the geometrical devices which her pots carry and with which she has made a counterpoint between form, colour and rhythm in the painting. The semi-familiarity of her forms provides an excellent foil for the emblematic aspect of their decoration.

An early example of the emblematic pot, *Floating Pillar* (1976) on page 36, is in reality a flattened jar. The profiles, the edges, of this jar are outlined with a painted line which looks like a square-section worm, while the central device, a single box in isometric projection, floats neither in nor on the pot, but somehow, somewhere, 'beyond' it. One might have touched this jar and as one did so had revealed before one's eyes a mysterious world – it would be like unlocking an aspect of nature at a touch.

Fritsch is, however, quick to disavow any suggestion that such painting as that in the example of the *Floating Pillar* pot should be regarded as decoration or ornament or pattern. One of the unfortunate consequences of the divisions between fine art and craft has been a downgrading of such roles and qualities as decoration and pattern. In recent years following the resurgence of interest in decoration among designers and architects, as well as artists, such words have regained some of their former dignity but a pejorative element still remains. To 'decorate' or to 'pattern' a pot implies too much that it is an addition which is not integral to the artefact as a whole. Whereas what Fritsch seeks is complete unity of the parts, image and form, rhythm of shape, rhythm of colour and line.

Fritsch is a perfectionist by nature and she works through improvisation. There is no contradiction here: just as a composer will begin to improvise, so Fritsch begins by randomly cutting the base for the pot and then building up the body of the pot with the form being dictated by the shape of the base. The difficult part is the last third of the pot: how to bring together the rhythms of the pot into a whole; it is a dialetic again between craftsmanship and spontaneity. The craftsmanship, the technical precision, is the necessary foundation to successful improvisation and yet it is an aspect which has to be second nature because the improviser's energies are directed towards a sucessful culmination of the work.

Fritsch and Veryan Weston once listed some of the parallels which formed the basis of their collaboration: these parallels included being unrepeatable – that is to say, improvised; hand-made and unmechanistic; intimate in scale and accessible; and technically prepared.

The formal qualities of Fritsch's work owe a lot to the conventions of good pottery. She is a good craftswoman, almost traditional, so that a conventional guide to what is good in pots can be used profitably in examining her work.

In *Style in Pottery*,[7] Arthur Lane said that good potting allows the clay to reveal its strength by making the walls no thicker than they need to be to support the pot, a skill that Fritsch has clearly acquired. In the 1984 pots there is a great variety of form but no hint of the lumpen. In the *Spout Pot* (1974) on page 46, we see quite a complicated construction, an architectural pot reminiscent of the rounded shell forms of Le Corbusier's chapel at Ronchamp (1950-55). An over-thickness of the walls of this pot would have been disastrous because so much depends upon the tidy transformation of one plane into another. It is also a squat pot, and an excess of clay would have turned it dumpy.

In common with most contemporary studio potters, Fritsch does not throw her pots on a wheel but coils and builds them up. This is important because it means that, on the whole, she is using not organic volumes but architectural ones.

By 'organic volume' I am referring particularly to thrown forms. A good thrown pot is one in which the volume seems to swell from inside – out and upwards; the form is upward in its movement, tense and yet still with an echo of its plasticity and the process of its swift growth from the wheel. Good throwing in contemporary Western societies is rare, perhaps because throwing is a peasant skill that not only takes years to learn but is best learnt and understood in a community of throwers – of people passing their knowledge on from one generation to another. Fluency is achieved in throwing when the skill becomes an act of intelligent intuition. Fritsch has achieved a fluency in her work but her work is more considered, more contemplative in its process than good intuitive throwing.

The predominance of flattish forms and planes can be explained in terms of Fritsch's interest in that '2½-dimensional optic', that sense of 'edge' which she has referred to. She has achieved success after success by breaking what can be regarded as a golden rule in pottery – one which Arthur Lane, for example, believed holds true for all painting on pottery: no ideas of space should be allowed to compete with the volume of the pot, which itself supplies all that is needed of the third dimension.

But not all Fritsch's pots emphasize flatness instead of volume: see, for example, *Spiral Jar* (1984) on page 33; *Spout Pot From Tlön* (1984) on page 79; and the various bowls she has produced. Each expresses a sense of volume. How is it achieved? Well, as Lane explains, the art of creating a sense of volume is partly bound in with suppressing the impact of a pot's profiles. So, if volume is the aim, one can remove handles and spouts because these items draw attention to profiles. Alternatively, horizontal lines can be used to reaffirm volume by bridging the gap between the profiles. You can also draw attention to the horizontal aspect at the base or neck of a pot (usually the narrowest parts) and this will create the effect of 'emphasizing the free curves between them'. Drawing attention to horizontal aspects can be done by lines, patterns or simply by making a precise kink in each profile. Look, for example, at *Vase* (1974) on page 61: the heavy emphasis upon the horizontal lines of the rim and the neck contribute to the sense of escape of the curves of the pot as they flow down and out and then under the pot. The painting, which moves diagonally across the surface, increases the sense of swelling by taking the eye around the pot's body – the painting is a continuation of the pot's rhythm.

The texture of the planes between the profiles is important. If the surface of a pot's body is smooth then the profiles are emphasized at the expense of volume. Fritsch does not use exaggerated texture, although the surfaces she makes are never smooth but painterly. The importance of this controlled texture has a lot to do with the 'charisma' that Fritsch admires in old frescoes. The metaphorical appeal of an old or ageless texture derives from her liking for the fiction that here we have pots that have been discovered rather than made recently. Quite often the effect of her painting is akin to scumbling – a technique used in oil painting in which an opaque colour is painted over another layer of a different colour in such a way that the bottom layer is not entirely obscured – which gives an effect of time and burial.

More often than not the texture of a Fritsch pot is in the rhythm she has painted. Demonstrating this aspect, a reminder of the analogy between pattern-reading and music is provided by what Lane said about ornament and surface: there are three principal rhythms that can emphasize the shape and volume of a pot. Firstly, there is the single punctuation mark (rarely used by Fritsch, but frequently used by potters such as Bernard Leach and by Korean, Chinese and Japanese potters). Secondly, there is the continuous frieze which leads the eye around the pot. Fritsch uses the logic of such a device to establish ambiguity as she does in *Optical Jar* (1976) on page 44, in which the broad bands of colour suggest a greater volume than the pot possesses.

Thirdly, there is the all-over repeating pattern which suggests continuity where the motifs narrow out in perspective to right and left.

One of the most dazzling displays of overall rhythm is to be found with *Quantum Pocket* (1984) on page 74 – a pot inspired by Borges's story *Death and the Compass*. Each cubic rectangle is different in size and has a different angle, being modified by the curvature of an imaginary space in relation to the actual curves of the pot. This is analogous in music to modifications in rhythm and tempo caused by the shape of a phrase or melodic line.

The spatial devices Fritsch uses are sometimes quite complicated and if you follow the rhythm on *Quantum Pocket* you can see an intriguing idea at work – the idea is to represent a plane, a space, folding over on itself. If you read from top right to bottom left the shapes are clearly defining a plane which bends: modern mathematics informs us that space can bend.

Now that some of the conventions have been established, it is appropriate to look at a pair of pots in detail. The first is *Crescendo Pot* (1976) on page 60. The shape of this piece demonstrates enormous care. Note the break in the line of each profile as it moves out from the neck. The two kinks set up the horizontal for us and we need this horizontal for a sense of stability or else we would, metaphorically speaking, lose our footing since everything else about this pot suggests an infinity of space and a lack of permanence. The broad stripes of dark and light green establish the flat plane of the pot, while the isometric boxes cast in perspective create the illusion of a vast (but folding) space. The profiles of the pot become a frame to a window, and the window opens into a different world. There is a sense of magic – it is like crystal-ball gazing.

The painting stops just a sliver short of each profile, and the edge that results from this acts as a hint to the eye that this painting is illusion on a flat plane. It is an interesting fact that art historians have noticed before that we seem to respond to illusion more strongly when we are reminded that it is an illusion. We appreciate the gap between the real and the unreal.

A crescendo is an increase in volume in music and so *Crescendo Pot* is a visual pun. The intensity of 'volume' is heightened by the pot's shape, which provides what Fritsch refers to as the 'dynamic' in her work. Note, too, the softness at the base, which provides a foil for the geometry of the painting. Soft/hard and light/shadow are visual devices which Fritsch uses a lot to give life to a pot.

The curved base is a common feature in Fritsch's work. She says the source of these curved bases derives from the notion of an interplay between earth and air, creating the sensation of lifting the vessel off the ground. It is one of the details which confirm the legitimacy of calling her work 'architectural'. One of the most important aspects in architecture is the interplay between light and shadow. By wrapping the plane well underneath itself so that the base disappears from sight, the resultant softened shadow tends to ooze like a mezzotint to create form.

These pots are designed to make you want to hold one in your hands, which in turn suggests that these are pots which are desirable and friendly to touch: and this is a strong part of their appeal.

Refinement of form is also an aspect of the pot's humanity. Look at the stately and imperious *Hexagonal Jar: From the Circular Ruins* (1984) on page 96. The refinement of this pot's form derives from such touches as the turn of the line into the base, the width and height of the rim, and the neatness and rightness of the angles at which the planes on this pot abut on to one another. Fritsch shows herself to be a master of composition with this pot: on the one hand the hexagonal form is strong and full of volume, the profiles pulled together in accordance with the Lane conventions, and, on the other hand, the geometric projections painted on the jar represent a different, other-worldly space and reality. There is no visual conflict between painting and form. A Fritsch pot always has repose. And here, with *Hexagonal Jar*, the spectator can easily hold the two realities – the real three-dimensional pot and the elusive ideal reality suggested by the geometric pattern – together in the mind. The balance between pot and painting and form and metaphor is absolutely right. There is also a fact not revealed by photography...Fritsch says: 'The pot is not functional although it is a real container, being fully vitrified and water-tight. But the pot's function is poetic, metaphoric, fictional.'[8]

Fritsch is a perfectionist in her work and her work is also the basis of a wider philosophy. She deplores the imprisonment of the imagination, of the individual's soul by late-twentieth-century materialism, 'I suppose it's an attempt to defy commodity values...it is this which drives me to turn each pot into something improvised and different and to squander days, even weeks on the making and painting of one vessel.'

A BIOGRAPHY

Elizabeth Fritsch studied ceramics at the Royal College of Art for four years. David Queensberry, Head of Ceramics, has written, 'During the years that Liz spent at the College she conducted hundreds of trials and tests in her search to get the right ceramic quality in her pots. Six months before her graduation she was still not getting the results she wanted. Then suddenly things began to improve. Nearly all the work that she submitted for her degree was produced in the last six months of her course.'

In a sense the determination to find the best results which marked her Royal College of Art career has coloured her professional life ever since. There have been relatively few solo exhibitions but each one of them has been important. In 1974 the then Crafts Advisory Committee (now the Crafts Council) gave her a solo exhibition and this brought her to the attention of the crafts world. In 1978 she had a major exhibition at the Leeds Art Gallery (Temple Newsam) – her famous 'Pots About Music' show.

In the early years of the 1980s Elizabeth Fritsch was busy looking after her young daughter, but at the end of 1984 there was an exhibition of new work: 'Pots From Nowhere', at the Royal College of Art.

Inevitably, since Fritsch's work is highly regarded and in short supply, it is both sought after and expensive and collectors have been quick to see the investment potential of her work. But to this Fritsch responds: 'I insist on museums having the first pick; I make pots for ordinary people.' There is no more fitting comment for an artist and a craftswoman to make.

1958-64   Studied harp and piano at the Royal Academy of Music.
1968-71   Studied at the Royal College of Art, awarded Silver Medal and Herbert Read Memorial Prize (1970).
1972   One-woman show in Copenhagen (Bing and Grondahl). Won major prize in Royal Copenhagen Porcelain Jubilee Competition.
1974   One-woman show at Waterloo Place Gallery, London (Crafts Advisory Committee). Contributor to Ceramic Forms (CAC and British Council touring exhibition); The Design Centre, London; Everyman a Patron (CAC); Towards Ceramic Sculpture (Oxford Gallery); One from Thirty, Amalgam, London.
1975   Two-woman show, with Anya Barnett, at Amalgam, London. Contributor to British Design exhibition, Mexico City; Kettles Yard, Cambridge.
1976   One-woman show at the British Craft Centre, London. Awarded Gold Medal at International Ceramics

Competition, Poland.
Contributor to British Ceramics,
Pennsylvania State University, USA.
1977   Contributor to Silver
Jubilee exhibition, V & A;
New Ceramics (Eastern Arts
Touring exhibition); Ceramics and
Textiles (British Council
exhibition touring Middle East);
'Say When', V & A; Crafts in
Question, Whitworth Art Gallery,
Manchester; Colour in Ceramics,
Midland Group, Nottingham;
Flavour of the '70s, Southampton
Art Gallery.
1978   One-woman show, Leeds
Art Galleries (Temple Newsam);
subsequently shown in Glasgow,
Bristol, Gateshead, Bolton and
London (V & A, 1979).
1979   Group Show, Warwick
Gallery, London.
1984   One-woman show, Royal
College of Art: 'Pots From
Nowhere'.

Public Collections
Kunst Industrie Museum,
Copenhagen.
Museum Boymans van Beuiningen,
Rotterdam.
Crafts Council London.
Leeds Art Galleries (Lotherton
Hall).
Victoria and Albert Museum,
London.
City Art Gallery, Bristol.
City Art Gallery, Manchester.

References
1. *Pots About Music* catalogue,
   Leeds Art Galleries, 1978.
2. Ibid.
3. *Ways of Seeing*, John Berger,
   Penguin, London, 1972.
4. *The Shock of the New*,
   Robert Hughes, BBC, London,
   1981.
5. *Pots About Music* catalogue,
   Leeds Art Galleries, 1978.
6. *The Sense of Order*,
   E H Gombrich, Phaidon,
   Oxford, 1979.
7. *Style in Pottery*, Arthur Lane,
   Faber, London, 1977.
8. All her pots are hand-built and
   painted with coloured slips.
   They are made from a grogged
   stoneware body, fired under
   oxidation to 1260°C, which
   renders them fully vitrified.

THE WORK

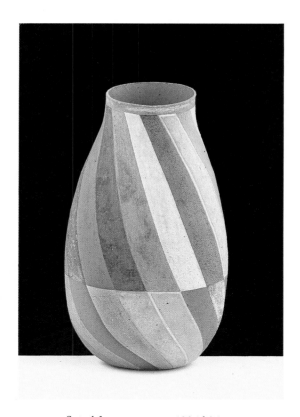

Spiral Jar, stoneware, 1984 h24cm

Top, Ethnic Bowl, stoneware, 1972 w26cm
Below, Ethnic Pot, stoneware, 1972 h16cm

Top, Ethnic Pot, stoneware, 1972 h16cm
Below, Ethnic Bowl, stoneware, 1972 w24cm

Top left, Group of three pots, stoneware, 1975-1978
Below left, Piano Jar, stoneware, 1978 h40cm
Top right, Floating Pillar, stoneware, 1976 h25cm
Below right, Jar with Floating Cubes, 1978 h40cm

Hexagonal Jar: From Nowhere Street , stoneware, 1984 h39cm.
Fritsch explains that 'Nowhere Street' is a haunting piece of
music by the composer and virtuoso soprano saxaphone player
Steve Lacey

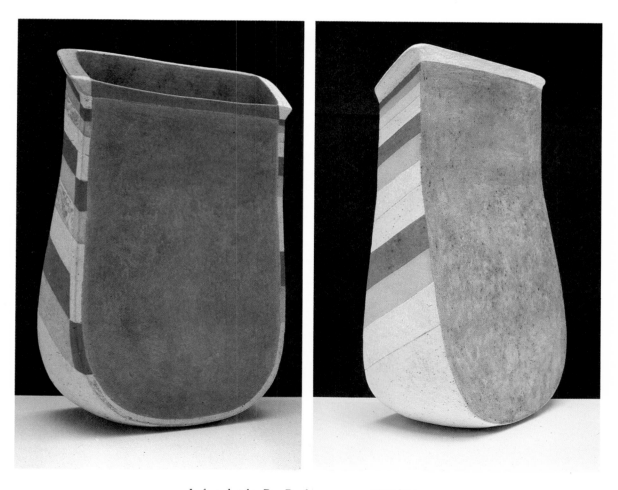

Left and right, Box Bottle, stoneware 1974 h24cm

Spout Pot, stoneware, 1974 h25cm

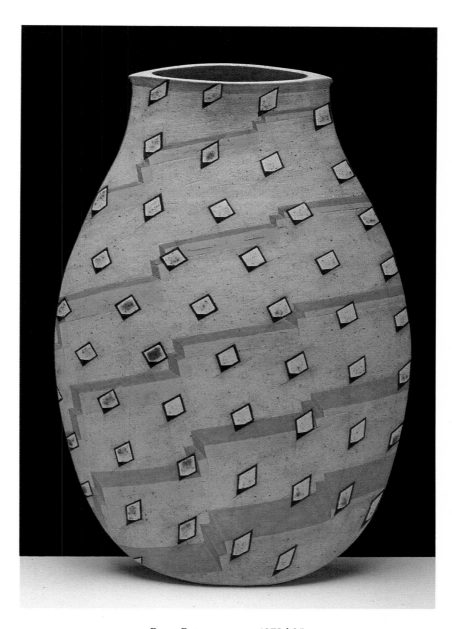

Piano Pot, stoneware, 1978 h35cm

Jar with Rhythm Figures in Counterpoint, stoneware,
1978 h35cm

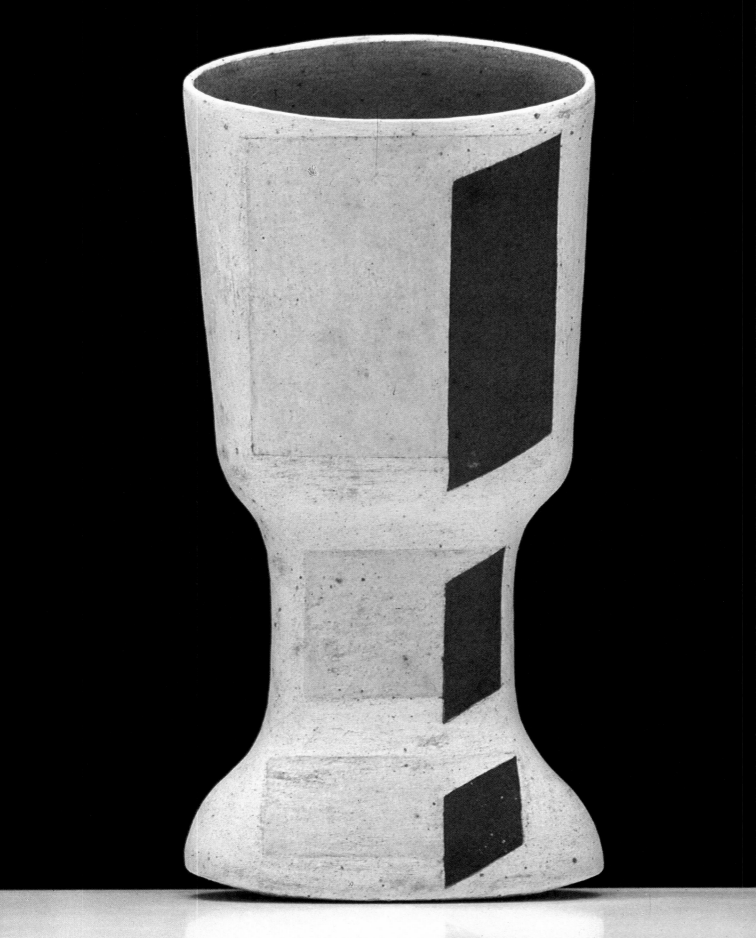

Floating Pillars, stoneware, 1975 h28cm. Fritsch uses painting and geometrical rhythms to transform the pot into a metaphorical object. Here the 'space' which is created by the floating pillars is made all the more potent – and surprising – for being contained by a jar. It hints at magic and science

Optical Cup, stoneware, 1975 h20cm

Left, Optical Jar, stoneware, 1976 h22cm
Right, Hexagonal Optical Jar, stoneware, 1976 h29cm

Optical Bottle, stoneware, 1976 h26cm. The side panels are
deliberately 'faded'

44

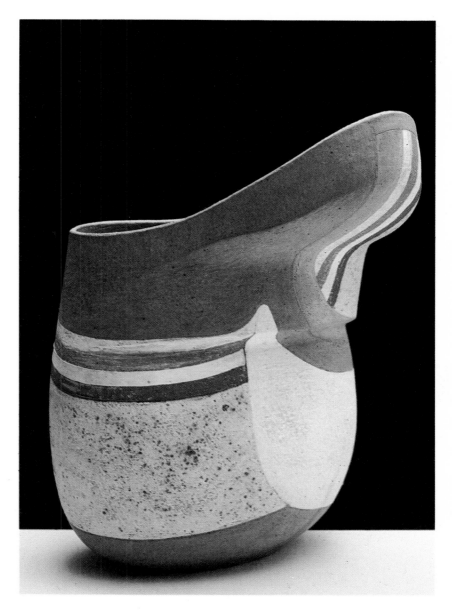

Spout Pot, stoneware, 1974 h24cm. This is reminiscent in its 'architecture' of Le Courbusier's forms at his chapel at Ronchamp, France

Above and preceding spread, Optical Pot with Pentatonic Cross Rhythms, stoneware, 1976 h32cm

Optical Vase with Cross Rhythms, stoneware, 1976 h28cm

Top left, Grey Bottle with Erosion, stoneware, 1984 h30cm
Top right, Piano Pot with Fractured Rhythmic Figures,
stoneware, 1978 h32cm
Below left, Spout Pot with Spiral, stoneware, 1976 h24cm
Below right, Spout Pot, stoneware, 1978 h24cm

Piano Pot with fractured Rhythm Figures, stoneware,
1978 h33cm

Jar with Triple Fractured Rim, stoneware, 1974 h14cm

Optical Pot, stoneware, 1975 h12cm

Left, Spout Pot, stoneware, 1974 h25cm
Right, Box Bottle, stoneware, 1975 h30cm

Optical Bottle, stoneware, 1975 h26cm

*Above and preceding spread, Crescendo Pot, stoneware, 1976.
Fritsch is very able at combining the rhythm of a pot's form with
a seemingly contradictory painting without subsuming the one to
the other. Here our eyes are led from the back to the front of an
illusionary space and then across and around as though space is
folding over itself — a theme which is developed in later pots.
The rounded, disappearing base of the pot makes the whole thing
appear to float*

*Vase, stoneware, 1974 h27cm. The heavy emphasis upon the
horizontal lines of the rim and the neck contribute to the sense of
escape of the pot's curves as they flow down and out and then
under the pot. The sense of the pot's volume swelling from within
is increased by the rhythm of painting which moves diagonally
across the pot*

Piano Pot with Cross Rhythms, stoneware, 1978 h30cm

*Counterpoint Jar, stoneware, 1975 h27cm. We see here a
combination of the swelling, 'organic' volume of the main body,
and the box-like, architectural volume of the neck. This is a
composition of harmony and contrast: emphatic horizontal rim
and neck vying with the soft oozing shadows around the base.
Yet again our eyes are deliberately led down and around the pot by
the rhythms of the painting. A pot to contemplate*

*Deep Bowl, stoneware, 1978 h21cm. With a wide, deep bowl
such as this one's instinct is to want to feel the interior as well as
the exterior form. Fritsch encourages this by giving the interior
surface a gently worn, soft appearance*

Deep Bowl, stoneware, 1978 h21cm. No contemporary British studio potter uses colour as vividly and yet as subtly as Fritsch. Her preference for a matt, fresco-like surface absorbs some of the light rather than bouncing it back callously as do so many modern machined products

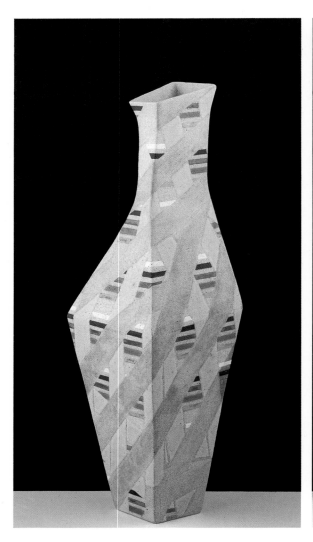 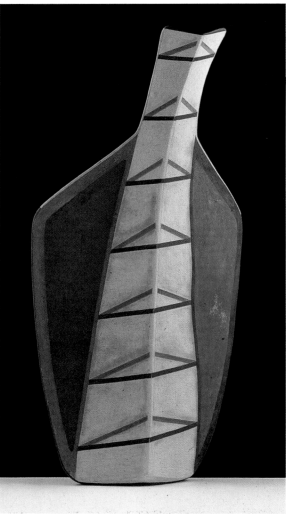

Left and previous spread (detail), Funeral Urn: from The Garden of Forking Paths, stoneware, 1984 h44cm. This is one of the pots from Fritsch's 'Pots from Nowhere' exhibition. The title refers to, although the pot does not illustrate, a story by Jorge Luis Borges. Fritsch comments, 'The rather hesitant, stuttering nature of these slats is a first attempt to express the Chinese music from the garden described by Borges: 'The stuttering sparks of the music continued upwards'
Right, Spout Pot with Ladder, stoneware, 1984 h53cm.

Large Flask, stoneware, 1984 h44cm

Two Cubist Jars, both 1984, h21cm, 28cm; Deep Basin with Spiral, 1984 h21cm

Jar from Tlön, stoneware, 1984 h30cm with Cubist Jar from the Fissure of a Dusty Aqueduct, stoneware, 1984 h21cm. Fritsch explains that with the cubist jar the subject – a pot – is no more than the pretext for a celebration of mathematical artifice and surprising colour

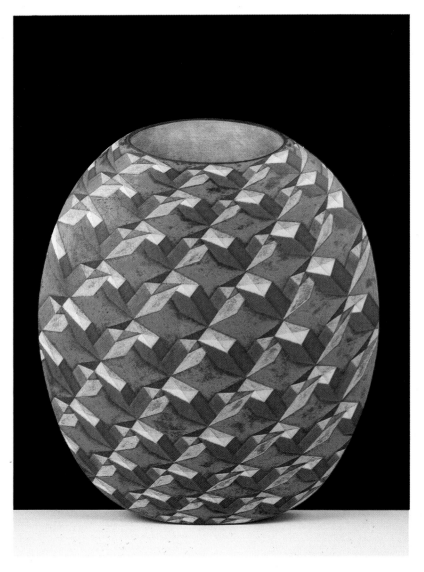

Above and previous spread, Quantum Pocket: from The Eucalyptus Garden of the Villa at Triste-Le Roy, stoneware, 1984 h31cm. This pot is a synthesis of several of the ideas which feed Fritsch's work: her interests in geometry, metaphysics and the surrealism contained in Borges's writings have all nurtured this pot. Here and in the preceding spread we can see that each cubic rectangle is slightly different, its shape being determined by the curves of the pot itself. The colours come from a metaphysician's palette – the ethereal blue voids are richly defined by brooding yellow ochres, greens and maroons. The smoky grey of the interior is a mystery

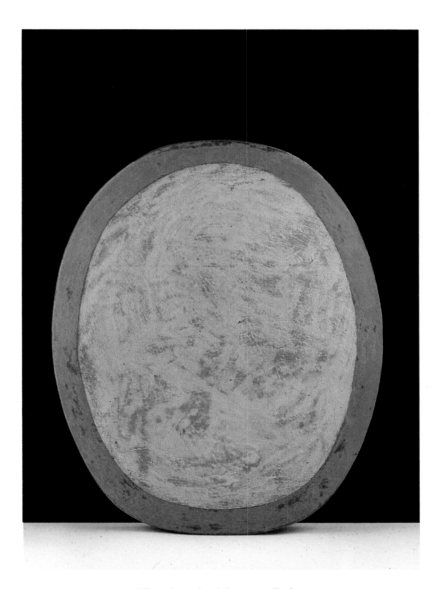

The other side of Quantum Pocket

Here and facing page, Moon Pockets, stoneware, 1976, 1984,
1975 h18cm

Three Spout Pots, stoneware, 1978-1979 h22cm, h28cm, h42cm

*Spout Pot from Tlön, stoneware, 1984 h29cm. Fritsch is right
when she speaks of this pot's 'hallucinatory light'*

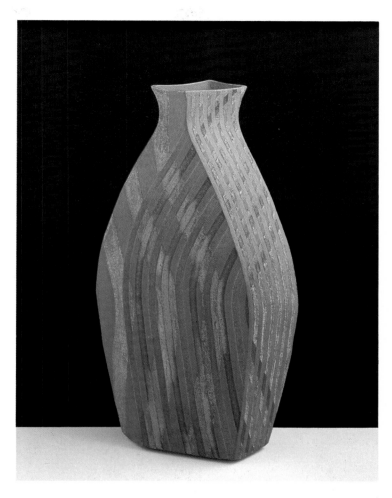

Above and facing page, Two Faced Jar, stoneware,
1984 h39cm

Left, Cubist Bottle, stoneware, 1984 h24cm
Right, Cubist Bottle, stoneware, 1984 h23cm
Facing page, Two Faced Jar, stoneware, 1984, h34cm

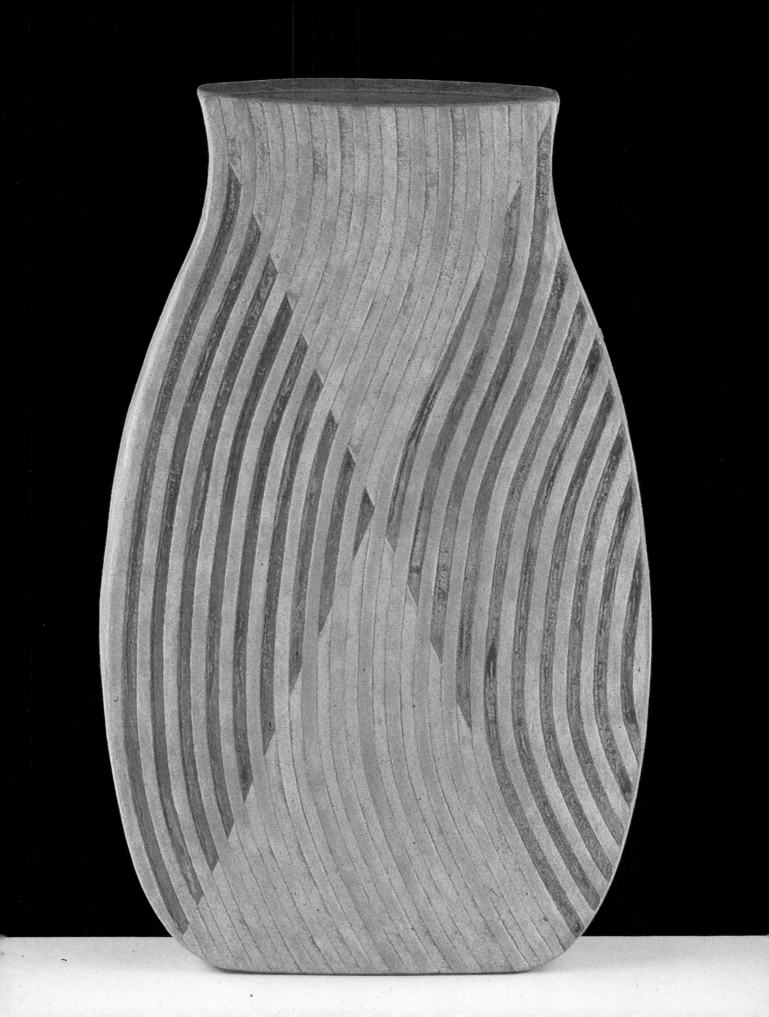

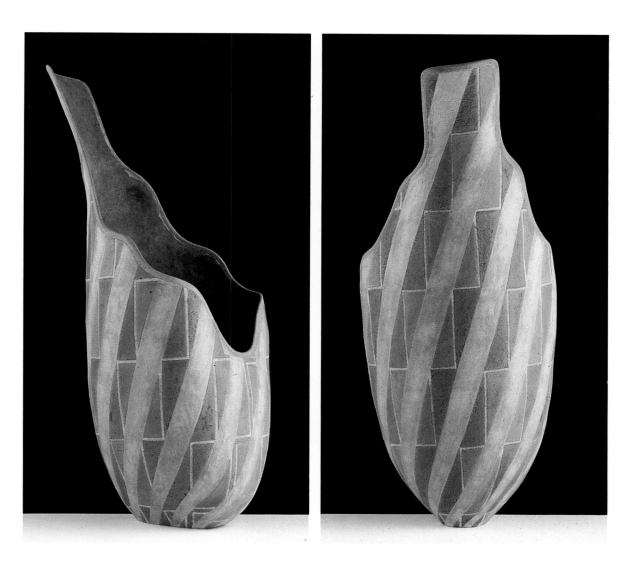

Left and right, Spout Pot, unfinished, stoneware, 1984 h44cm

Funeral Urn – Windblown, stoneware, 1984 h31cm

Piano Pots, stoneware, 1978 greatest height 32cm
Facing page, Flattened Bottle with Counterpoint and Cross
Rhythms, stoneware, 1978 h34cm

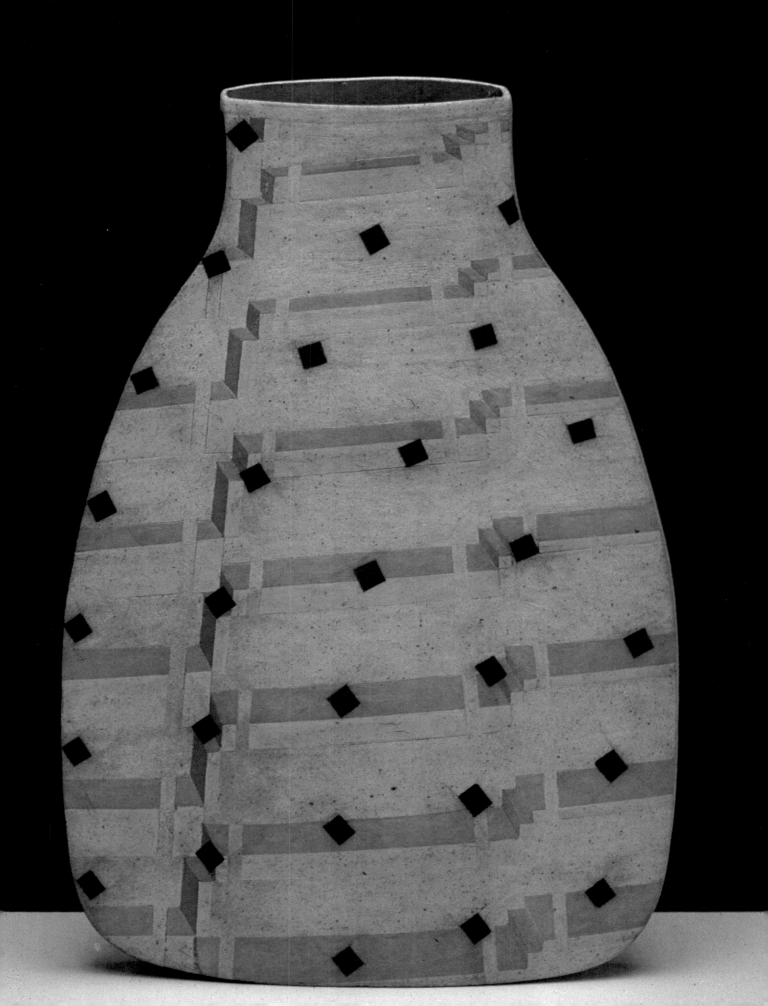

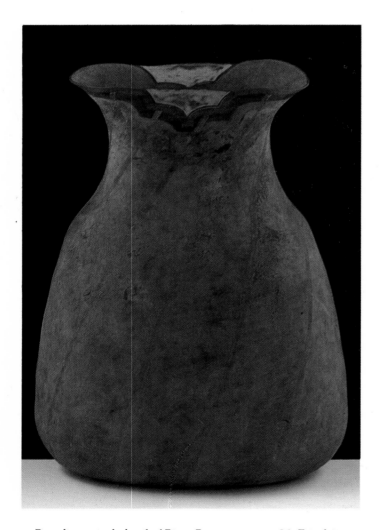

*Preceding spread, detail of Piano Pot seen on page 86. Fritsch is
in some respects a miniaturist, like Paul Klee. The elegance of the
composition of the detail grows apparent with successive views.
Above, Terraqueous Jar with Erosion, stoneware, 1984 h38cm
Facing page, Flattened Bottle, stoneware, 1978 h28cm*

Cubist Jar, stoneware, 1984 h28cm

Cubist Jar, stoneware, 1984 h28cm

Above and preceding spread, Hexagonal Jar: From the Circular Ruins, stoneware, 1984 h37cm. This is an ample demonstration that Fritsch's pots are poetic, metaphoric and fictional – the pot 'works' by referring to both the real world of objects and another world, which might be fictional or that other, mathematical, world where physicists and mathematicians and musicians play. Fritsch uses geometry as metaphor, not applied pattern

INDEX

Anglo-orientalism 12
architectural 30

Bauhaus 9
Blake, William 14
Borges, Jorge Luis 18,19,22,29
Brancusi, Constantin 8
Breton, André 17
Berger, John 15,16

Cardew, Michael 10
Coper, Hans 8,10-12,13
craft, definition of 7-9,11
Crafts Council 13
decoration 13,26
dialectic 8,17

function 8,25,30

games 19
geometry 13-14,17,25
Gombrich, E.H. 23,24
Holbein, Hans 15-16

ideal art 22
illusion 13
improvisation 24,26

Kandinsky, Wassily 22

Lacey, Steve 22
Lane, Arthur 26,27,28,30
Le Corbusier 27
Leach, Bernard 20,28
Lucie-Smith, Edward 18

Malevich, Kasimir 23
metaphysics 17,18
music 22,23,24

Oriental 11,24

painting 28
Paolozzi, Eduardo 12
perspective 13

Queensberry, David 11

Rie, Lucie 10,11,12
Royal Academy of Music 11,22
Royal College of Art 12,29
rhythm 23

surreal 8,13,14,17,18,25
synaesthesia 22

throwing 27

volume 13,27

Weston, Veryan 23,26